OUR FAMILY FARM

Written by Abena Eyeson
Illustrated by Kofi Ofosu

Contents

Welcome! 3
Off to the farm 5
Weather in Ghana 9
Our crops 10
Fruit or vegetable? 12
The nursery 13
The greenhouses 17
The tomato greenhouse 18
The cucumber greenhouse 21
The bell pepper greenhouse 22
Where it all goes! 23
Glossary and Index 24

OXFORD
UNIVERSITY PRESS

Words to look out for …

current (*adjective*)
happening or used now

discard (*verb*)
discards, discarding, discarded
to get rid of something because it is useless or unwanted

proof (*noun*)
a fact or thing that shows something is true

reject (*verb*)
rejects, rejecting, rejected
To reject something is to get rid of it.

urgent (*adjective*)
needing to be done or dealt with immediately

whereas (*verb*)
but, or on the other hand

Welcome

Hello! My name is Ama. I'm nine years old and I live in Ghana, West Africa. I live with my parents, my nana, and my little brother, Kojo.

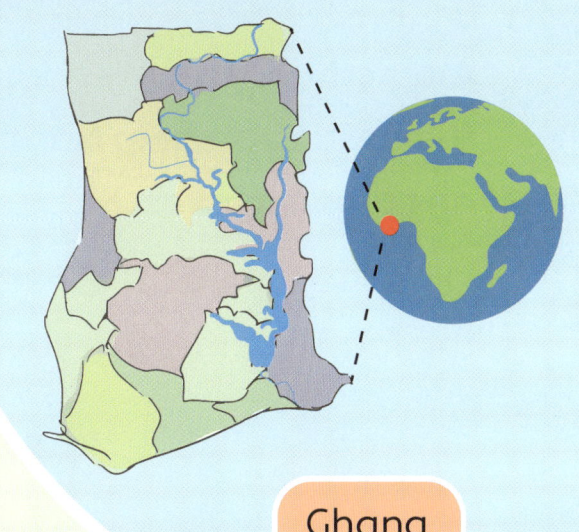

Ghana

our house

me

Mum

Kojo

Dad

Nana

Our house is special because it's right next to our farm.

After school, I do my homework. I like maths the best. I also help Nana and Kojo with any urgent chores.

Once I've finished, I can go off and explore the farm. Let me give you a tour!

Urgent means needing to be done or dealt with immediately.

Off to the farm

Our farm is located just outside Accra (say: uh-krah), Ghana's capital city. We grow lots of things in huge **greenhouses**.

greenhouses

Ghana

Accra

I hope to run the farm one day, just like my parents. Maybe Kojo will help me!

My parents had always dreamed of having a farm. Dad used to work with computers and Mum worked in a bank. However, neither of them could <u>discard</u> their dream.

Since they bought the land, our farm has grown and grown. You'll see!

To <u>discard</u> something is to get rid of it because it is useless or unwanted.

Here's Fifi and Jojo! They help to keep the farm secure with Emmanuel, our guard. The dogs mainly like to play though!

Emmanuel welcomes people to the farm. He also checks that all the farm's tools are kept safe.

This is Mum's office. She likes to work at her desk whereas Dad prefers to be on the farm.

Mum has lots of plans for the farm! She's always thinking of ways we can grow more food.

Anyway, I'm not usually allowed in here. Let's go!

Whereas means but, or on the other hand.

Weather in Ghana

Ghana is a **tropical** country so it's often hot here, but we have two rainy seasons. The hot weather makes it ideal for growing things.

The current season is called **harmattan** (say: har-muh-tan). Harmattan is very dry and dusty.

If something is current, it is happening or used now.

Our crops

You're probably wondering what we grow on the farm.

Our main **crops** are tomatoes, cucumbers and bell peppers. They love the sun! We can grow lots and lots of them.

This room is filled with crops from a recent **harvest**.

Green peppers aren't ripe yet, <u>whereas</u> red, yellow, and orange ones are.

Did you know there are many different kinds of tomato? We grow the most popular kinds.

Cucumbers are popular in Ghana and in other countries. They are used in lots of recipes.

<u>Whereas</u> means but, or on the other hand.

Fruit or vegetable?

Some people think we grow vegetables. Actually, they are all fruits!

See the seeds inside this tomato? That is the proof. Fruit comes from flowering plants and usually contains seeds.

seeds

Vegetables are the leaves, stem, or roots of a plant.

12 Proof is a fact or thing that shows something is true.

The nursery

Here's Dad! He's in the plant **nursery**. This is where plants are grown until they are ready to be moved to the greenhouses.

Dad makes sure the young plants get the right amount of sunlight, water and **fertilizer**.

The plants grow from tiny seeds that we plant in the soil.
Sometimes Dad lets me help him take care of them.
I have to be very careful because the seedlings
are **fragile**.

seedlings

seed tray

Kofi, Yaa and Mary are waving at us. They work on the farm when Mum and Dad need their help.

Sometimes, I help by watering the plants. I have my own special watering can!

These young plants are big enough to be moved now. Kofi, Yaa and Mary will help Dad plant them in the greenhouses.

Dad checks all the seedlings first. He <u>rejects</u> the damaged and unhealthy ones.

bell pepper plants

cucumber plants

tomato plants

16 To <u>reject</u> something is to get rid of it.

The greenhouses

Using greenhouses means we can grow crops all year long, even in rainy weather.

This is Esi. She is a soil expert. She visits the farm to tell Dad what the soil needs. Today she is taking some soil to test in her lab.

Esi

The tomato greenhouse

Have you ever tried growing a plant? You probably grew it in soil or **compost**.

In our greenhouses, we don't always use ordinary soil. We use cocopeat (say: coh-coh-peet). This is a special soil made from part of a coconut called the husk.

coconut husk

cocopeat

Tomato plants need lots of water! Cocopeat holds on to the water well, so the plants don't dry out.

Cocopeat also allows air to flow through it. This stops the roots from rotting.

We grow all our plants upwards so more light can reach the leaves. This way we can grow more, too!

Look at this tomato flower. Inside each flower is a berry. The berry grows until it's a tomato. It ripens, changing colour from green to red.

The cucumber greenhouse

Cucumbers also grow from flowers, but they stay green when they ripen.

Greenhouse cucumbers are long and smooth. Cucumbers grown outdoors are shorter, with bumpy skin. Next time you see a cucumber, see if you can tell if it was grown in a greenhouse!

The bell pepper greenhouse

Bell peppers grow out of a flower, like tomatoes and cucumbers. They start out green but turn yellow, orange or red when they are ripe. However, people like to eat them when they're green, too.

The red ones are my favourite. They taste sweet!

Our fruit is sold to restaurants, shops and market sellers. Mum is planning to make canned tomatoes soon.

Nana also uses our fruit to make her special tomato and bell pepper pies. Actually, it's time for our snack now. It's been great showing you around!

23

Glossary

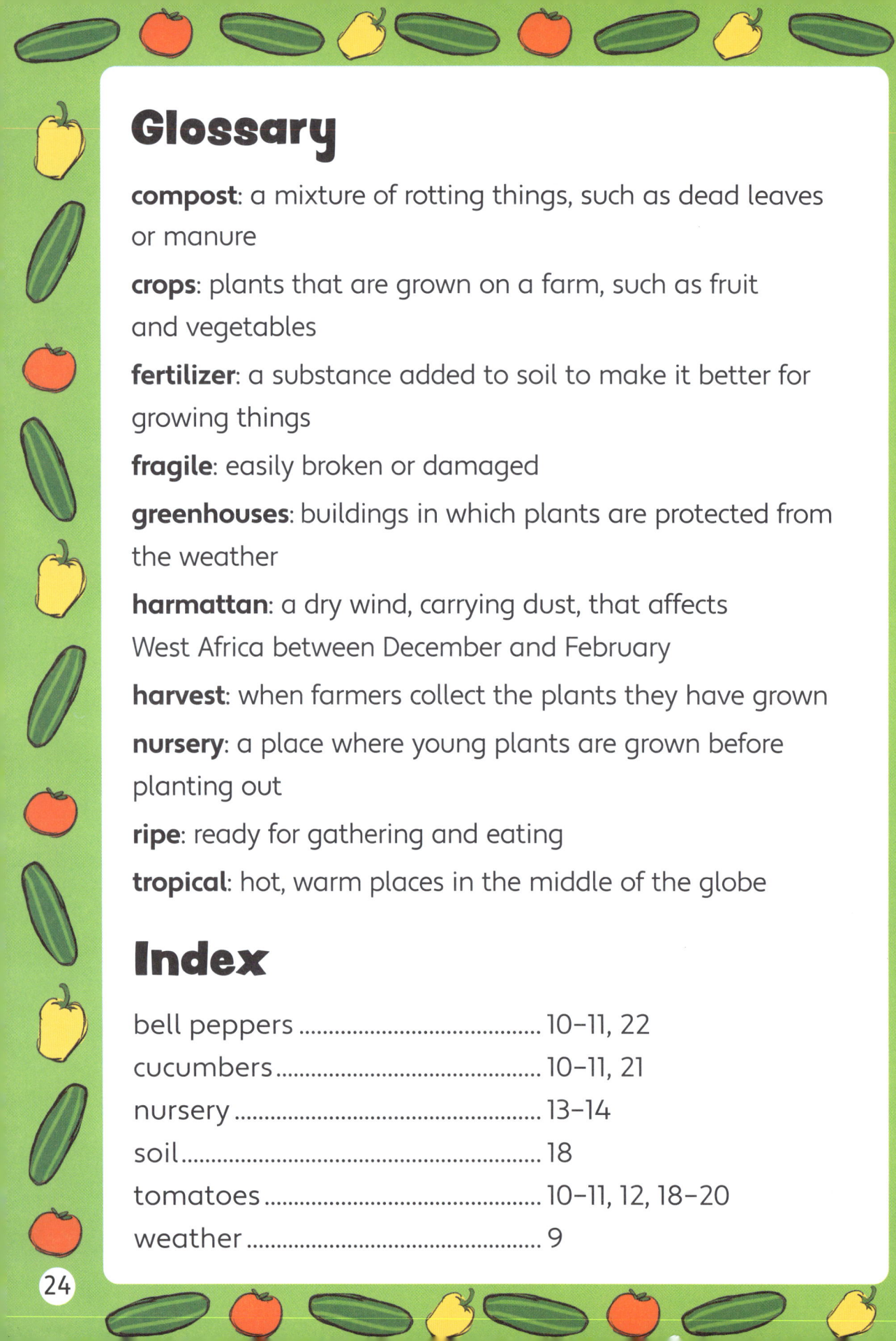

compost: a mixture of rotting things, such as dead leaves or manure

crops: plants that are grown on a farm, such as fruit and vegetables

fertilizer: a substance added to soil to make it better for growing things

fragile: easily broken or damaged

greenhouses: buildings in which plants are protected from the weather

harmattan: a dry wind, carrying dust, that affects West Africa between December and February

harvest: when farmers collect the plants they have grown

nursery: a place where young plants are grown before planting out

ripe: ready for gathering and eating

tropical: hot, warm places in the middle of the globe

Index

bell peppers	10–11, 22
cucumbers	10–11, 21
nursery	13–14
soil	18
tomatoes	10–11, 12, 18–20
weather	9